SHIA LaBEOUF

AK BLAKEMOR

4   *hollywood*

6   *Shia LaBeouf*

8   *the reading*

9   *pilates*

10   *Aurora, Mile End*

12   *sparrow's wet dream*

14   *Diana, lonely*

15   *tourmaline*

16   *Love's Easy Tears*

18 >

30 *may*

32 *tiny violetflavoured*

34 *the evening sun licks a single tear*

35 *something like, i forgive everything*

36 *destroyer*

37 *fantasy*

38 *co-star*

hollywood

i am:

pigs walking in the shadow
along the beaches where the bodies wash up
clothed in iridescent paillettes.

sometimes quieter -
a drinking spider.

but listen
i could also be very big

a thing people will not understand
once i am dead.

Shia LaBeouf

the closest i have ever been to actor and performance artist Shia LaBeouf was a night in the winter of 2012 when LaBeouf was involved in an altercation at south London pub The Hobgoblin, after a stranger tried to steal his trucker cap. despite the multiple proven cases of plagiarism that have dogged his creative practice - and an apparent propensity for emotional and even violent outbursts – i harbour a real affection for Shia, whose recent work appears to demonstrate a self-parodic bonhomie. i remember with fondness his puckish antics in the role of Louis Anthony Stevens, anathema to his family of suburban California over-achievers. as with Lindsay Lohan, his face has become the locus of a nostalgia whose dimensions are not merely temporal, but also geographic:
for a second world of heat shimmer in the rich air over football fields / food processors / suntanned fathers & the sylph-like tragedians of lyme disease.

i like his 'CREEPER' stomach tatt. how he bled the eccentricities of his own celebrity persona to produce an electrifying performance in American Honey. the whimsical attenuation of a professional apology delivered via skywriting, puffs of abasement on hammered blue

if you're reading this, Shia, you've an advocate and friend in me

8

the reading

shivering cock!
dedicate a bad poem to William Faulkner
& also your mother

pilates

in the park -
vs. geranium dawn

grown-ass men
gather at the iron gates to watch

with the large sleepy feet
of wilderness saints

Aurora, Mile End

and it's Aurora
ornery in conversation
reflected in
a crosswise salver
between the lines
no little boy needs her
alive. lovely arms
like the struts belonging to an instrument
of martian origin - fields of opal-grain -

speculatively re-assembled yet
tragically unplayed.

sparrow's wet dream

morning chores
as hot as a penance
—derette - stationery - grocery
all the products i love
wanna stamp on something expensive
for sex reasons

yellow mango in blue mesh bag
the colour of bird-eating spiders

lissom mind
in little naked restraints –

13   is spite factory.
there's a crowd around the carousel
a cluster of secret misdeeds and taffy loops
of outraged light
desire
fallows me

here i dream awake of
your treasured
senior meat

Diana, lonely

male models in distressed jeans
dance to Roxy Music

moon
peeping down on the veranda
from her supratarsal turquoise
amorous, tear-streaked –

tourmaline

good bad girl
tell me i can't and i'll
embarrass you

the moon rolls over our lovemaking
like the clean eye
of an apex predator
tourmaline:

      parallel and elongated
      acicular prisms
      sometimes radiating
      massive, scattered

Love's Easy Tears

there's more to life than
boys/cathexis.

i fantasise
Lalique presents me with three raindrops
on a square of raw moose velvet –
(he calls these *Love's Easy Tears*)

or Elsa Hosk
in the 2018 Fantasy Bra
her Swedish nudity
evoking the abeyant spangle
of vacant skating rinks.

17

we kiss.

google
how to hide a cigarette burn
with a string of pearls.

if given licence
my own frailty
will become voluble -
bioluminescent.

think
wet hair and
fabulous ardour -
knuckles
taste of blood
and lemon rind.

i will not diet
but *curate*
between my thighs

this negative space.

sorry i don't understand
phenomenology

to temper my libido
i sometimes think of Martin Shkreli

your hand
in my polyblend running shorts
milk of poppy

19   >

retailing
single 'dead swan'
in white medical-grade silicone

>

if i died would it somehow
expose you?

your cult heroes on video
masturbating in front of underage girls
at house parties and other such
mundane *amours* -

i look at women on public transport
and wonder if you would find them attractive
it makes the misery uncurl so sweetly

21　　　　like a satin glove
or (with my apologies) *rosebud*
with that boast of the wholesome in
ductile pink courtine and
microtransactions
of morning dew

>

look how i quake
at visual cue –
portrait of a fuckboy
eating cotton candy

frangible leaf /
snakeskin shoe

all my fountains are in thee

trove of middle-child
when has your skin ever been other
than perfect?

my life
begs you fix it
as the rains tear rotten inflorescence
from the parasol tree -

\>

beating him off in the shower
is gloomy

like night visitations
from an aphasiac doll –
the withheld forgiveness
of my silverfish

and what really mattered
were the cancers we metastasised
along the way!

skinny throat behind
suburb's water-colour fascia -
blood spotted on the guest pillows.

the other afternoon
i almost whistled after the hatchet-faced man
on his big red bicycle
like
pursue me!

27   the icicles
in crackling fantasia from wingmirror -
too many times left dry.

i like the girl in her leopard print coat
with the boy outside the takeaway
i sincerely hope they fuck
have great respect

my god
like a fool I Hold You
it continues it continues

your shyness
warrants respect

this leather couch
my catafalque – Midnight Train to Georgia &
winsome vaping. daddy's little hammer. sucks
to be bodies in space. autocomplete

does soul last forever

may

a sun poem. the happy roach
sloughs off his blue skin –

a fat bee on a bright brick wall.

we roll apart
our grave-beds loose and hot

adrift
on salpodeine &
the atrocious swan of love

so many bouquets
it's like somebitch died –

31   using affection
as a bulwark
against modernity's axiomatic selfishness
which i realise may after all be my great theme like
fuck

tiny violetflavoured

here i am of sunday
and earth rotoxid – fortunate
for all i am not very giving of myself.

the mad winds in trees behind the houses and
indulgent babies

i'm bad
but better than Lars von Trier

like depression
all your friends have had me

33   affirmation: even the slug (who is most profane)
trails a platinum appliqué
of artistic tragedy

the evening sun licks a single tear

by the boating lake
the evening sun licks a single tear
from the face of a red-headed child.

can we get out more?
your personal beauty - though great -
has become

seems, now, touchingly inadequate -

something like, i forgive everything

as i said, all i wanted this morning was to climb back into bed
with you. the sunshine was bright and grasses
were coming, exquisitely.
i felt it necessary almost
to recover, let the day in.

there –
there is a whole gala of care in me
on seeing your wrist bent
in sleep's amniotic reach

who is this girl standing at a window
wanting sprinklers to rain down lovely on hot skin,
with all the *joie de vivre* thereby
implied

destroyer

there was a silence when i told him i was *better*. a silence
as he considered

how *better than him* was what i considered
myself to be. and on a sunday afternoon, golden. the hour
one might make a a daughter sit down to practice
at her grand piano

fantasy

each morning
many cats
on my slick lawn -

pink-winged
and white as supplements
serving as prankish rebuke
to puberty

co-star

Try to leap before looking.

It is a good day to cast a spell.

You don't know enough about anything to write a book about it - apart from, perhaps, that sense of unfulfilled longing. Desire for what will ultimately hurt you.

You have to believe in something.

You have to take care of your own wellbeing.

Your intellectual insecurity will inhibit you. You fear that others will detect it, in the rarefied social circles in which you sometimes move - like a body odour.

39   Shoplift earrings from Urban Outfitters.

You walk down the street in platform shoes. Your aunt is in a coma. The trees - they know what they know about whatever.

Your anger is a small child whose opinions and feelings were never validated.

You will implicate the reader.

Go out tonight.

Your are an intern. Your impecunity will force you to duck into hotels on the way into work, and steal pastries from the continental breakfast spreads. Slices of grapefruit on white ice, black coffee.

You've been pronouncing it wrong for years.

40   Are you hungry, angry, lonely or tired?

You miss him sometimes – which seems an improvement on the *at all times* you were expecting.

Feel everything.

You must support your friends through their own suffering. The girls are bent over the bar like daisies with dark blue hearts.

Enfold yourselves in affordable luxury. The firebird spines of gladioli.

Emptiness leaves a way open for grace.

A K Blakemore is the author of two full-length collections of poetry: *Humbert Summer* (Eyewear, 2015) and *Fondue* (Offord Road Books, 2018), which was awarded the 2019 Ledbury Forte Prize for Best Second Collection. She has also translated the work of Sichuanese poet Yu Yoyo (My Tenantless Body, Poetry Translation Centre, 2019). Her poetry and prose writing has been widely published and anthologised, appearing in the The London Review of Books, Poetry, Poetry Review and The White Review, among others. She is currently working on her debut novel, which will be published in Spring 2021 by Granta.

Other titles available in the *New Words* series:
Livia Franchini: *Our Available Magic*
Alanna McArdle: *split ends / rooms*
Eloise Hendy: *the blue room*
Angus Carlyle: *Night Blooms*
MIDDEX: *Perpetual Skip*
Maike Hale-Jones: *There's always change at...*

SHIA LaBEOUF

First published in the UK in 2020 by Makina Books

makinabooks.com

Edited by Robin Christian
Designed by Patrick Fisher of Frontwards Design
Distributed by Cornerhouse Publications, Manchester

ISBN 978-1-9160608-6-9

A record for this book can be found at the British Library

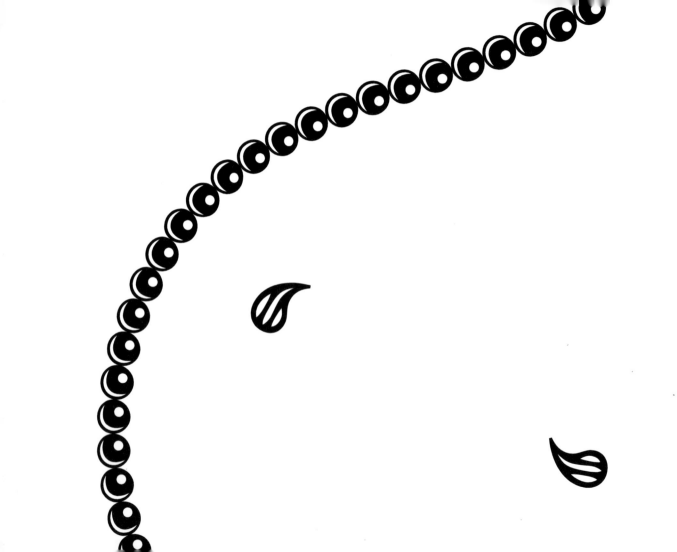